BENEDICT SHEEHAN
VESPERS

for soloists and SATB choir unaccompanied

OXFORD
UNIVERSITY PRESS

OXFORD
UNIVERSITY PRESS

Great Clarendon Street, Oxford OX2 6DP,
United Kingdom

Oxford University Press is a department of the University of Oxford.
It furthers the University's objective of excellence in research, scholarship,
and education by publishing worldwide. Oxford is a registered trade mark of
Oxford University Press in the UK and in certain other countries

First published 2022

Impression: 1

ISBN 978-0-19-356071-0

Music origination by Stephen Lamb
Text origination by Katie Johnston

Printed in Great Britain on acid-free paper by
Halstan & Co. Ltd, Amersham, Bucks.

Contents

Composer's Introduction

In the beginning God created the heaven and the earth. And the earth was without form, and void; and darkness was upon the face of the deep. And the Spirit of God moved upon the face of the waters. And God said, Let there be light: and there was light. And God saw the light, that it was good: and God divided the light from the darkness. And God called the light Day, and the darkness he called Night. And the evening and the morning were the first day.

—*Genesis 1: 1–5*

Synthesis

The story of *Vespers*—a choral setting of the evening office of the Orthodox Church—begins about six years ago with a simple proposal from Fr. Sergius, abbot of St. Tikhon's Monastery and my longtime friend and employer, that I write a Vespers based on traditional Russian chant. 'Like Rachmaninoff,' he said.

My *Vespers* is, first and foremost, a synthesis of chant and my own background and musical inheritance, a piece at once arising from the Orthodox tradition and situated solidly within the currents of my own life. As a son of Anglo–Irish–Scottish–French–Dutch–American converts to Eastern Orthodoxy, I'm no stranger to the notion of synthesis. At least as it exists today in North America and Europe, Orthodoxy is itself the product of synthesis, a panoply of ethnic traditions and ecclesiastical cultures that have been forced into contact with one another—and with countless other religious traditions besides—in modern pluralistic societies. Russian, Greek, Syrian, Lebanese, Ukrainian, Romanian, Albanian, Georgian, Indian, Armenian, Ethiopian (the list goes on): all are united primarily by a common creed and a shared (though richly varied) set of liturgical rites. The music in many Orthodox parishes naturally reflects this diversity, especially in the English-speaking American congregations in which I grew up and in which I still work today. My piece, therefore, can be seen as an attempt to honor and legitimize this diversity within Orthodoxy, as well as to create an artistic vision of unity that can be expanded upon, both in my own work and through the work of others.

The work of synthesis is difficult, though, both culturally and musically. Diversity is inherently complicated and can often represent a frustrating obstacle to efficiently achieving goals. However, I find that struggling for unity in a way that leaves inherent complexity intact ultimately renders much more satisfying solutions than holding to an abstract notion of unity under whose sway all complexity must either conform or be eliminated. This has become for me a governing philosophy. One of the specific ways this philosophy manifests itself musically in my *Vespers* is the frequent use of irregular-meter chant melodies. For me, finding a chant that refused to fit into either regular time-signatures or symmetrical phrase lengths was an exciting challenge and nearly always generated interesting and unexpected musical results. Thus were born 'The Opening Psalm', 'Blessed is the man', 'Rejoice, O Virgin', and 'The Closing Psalm', all of which are based on rhythmically knotty chants from the medieval Slavic tradition and none of which, to my knowledge, had ever been arranged before. If a melody wouldn't fit into a box, I let the melody create its own uniquely shaped container.

Arising out of this, I also took as paradigmatic the inherent rhythmic irregularity of the liturgical texts. Given that every word in *Vespers* (at least as presented here in English translation) is essentially blank verse or prose, rigid metrical treatment of the text seemed to me to be out of place. This is especially evident in the soloist parts in 'The Opening Psalm', 'Great Litany', and 'The Trisagion Prayers'—where I went about as far as I could towards notating the actual rhythms of speech—as well as in the trio sections of 'Blessed is the man' and the semi-choruses of 'The Lamp-lighting Psalms'. Maybe it's because I'm a lifelong stutterer, and thus acutely aware of both the immense complexity and elusive beauty of speech rhythms, that I find the rhythmic patterns of the spoken word so endlessly fascinating. My love affair with rap, the poetry of Gerard Manley Hopkins, and Konnakol (which I only recently discovered) may also have something to do with it. Whatever the reason, I chose in my *Vespers* to treat the inherent rhythmic complexity of the text as a body of musical riches to be synthesized within a larger rhythmic structure rather than as a thing to be purified of inconsistencies and forced into regular barlines and periods. This is not to say anything against texts that are neatly metered to begin with—I love those too and will happily set them to music—but rather to say that my approach is largely one of accepting things as I find them and then seeing what arises.

Psalmody and Chiastic Structure

The core of vespers, as of all the daily offices, is the singing of psalms. The cycle of psalms sung at appointed hours of the day establishes the fundamental rhythm of monastic services going back at least to the third century of the Christian era. Psalms are often called the 'backbone' of Orthodox services. Like an actual backbone, however, they are frequently ignored in daily practice. Oftentimes in Orthodox services today psalms are either chanted on a monotone by a solo reader or extensively abbreviated or even omitted altogether in favor of changeable hymnography. Thus, one of my conscious goals in composing *Vespers* was to place a renewed emphasis on the singing of psalms.

Using my late father's wonderful translations, I delved into the vespers psalms, and, in particular, into the psalms' chiastic structure. Chiastic structure is an ancient poetic device named for the Greek letter *chi* (X) and employed throughout the psalms as well as in many books of the Bible. Loosely defined, it functions a little like a palindrome where the first line of a section is mirrored by the last, the second by the second to last, and so on towards a center-point. According to my father, who studied and wrote about chiastic structure extensively, the center-point may not be the exact numerical middle of a psalm—he explained to me once that it is frequently offset a little towards the end (which starts sounding suspiciously like the Golden Mean to me [0.618])—but that every psalm has a line somewhere near the middle, or a little past it, that casts light both forward and backward in the psalm. For a composer, a large-scale structural concept like this offers irresistible insights, both into the formal organization of a text, as well as into its layers of meaning. (Bach and Brahms, incidentally, were also famously interested in chiastic structure.) I used a chiastic approach to a significant extent in organizing the two longest movements of *Vespers*, 'The Opening Psalm' and 'The Closing Psalm'.

Once I began thinking chiastically, though, it was hard to stop, and so it gradually became evident to me that *Vespers* itself could be organized along chiastic lines. Thus, 'The Opening Psalm' and the musically related 'Closing Psalm' emerged to form the bookends of the piece, with 'The Lamp-lighting Psalms'/'Stikhira of the Resurrection' and 'The Lord is King' surrounding the (slightly off-center) center-point of 'O gladsome Light'. Though not a psalm itself, *O gladsome Light (Φῶς Ἱλαρόν, Lumen Hilare)*—which proclaims Jesus to be the 'gladsome Light of the holy glory of the immortal Father'—is the earliest known Christian hymn still in common use and has effectively been the 'theme-song' of vespers for the entire history of Christianity. Realizing that *O gladsome Light* was also the chiastic heart of vespers—something I think I had sensed intuitively from long years in church—I saw that *light*, and in particular, *light from darkness*, was somehow thematic of vespers as a whole.

Light from Darkness

Vespers is, significantly, the beginning of the liturgical day in Orthodoxy, not the end of it. Just as the world emerged—or rather, say the particle physicists that I've been reading about lately, continually *emerges*—out of the darkness of non-being, so the Christian liturgical day begins each evening with the setting of the sun. At the risk of waxing philosophical, allow me to observe here that what perhaps seems at first glance to be an accident of liturgical scheduling becomes upon closer inspection a powerful existential symbol, and one, moreover, that sends out threads of connection deep into the realms of cosmology, biology, quantum mechanics, and human psychology. Almost on a daily basis I ask myself, *Where does this infinite universe and all its matter come from? Where do I come from, and why do I exist at all? Where do my thoughts come from, and why are they so often irrational?* Underneath such questions, at least for me, lies a veritable ocean of darkness and my own tiny lights almost always seem comically incapable of illuminating any of it. And yet at the same time within these unsettled depths there also seems to me to be something, or perhaps some*one*—a presence, a mind, a voice—that says gently, but with tireless insistence, 'Let there be light'. And behold, for no apparent reason, there *is* light—there is meaning, there is form, there is personhood, there is consciousness—and not only *is* it, but it is *good*.

For me as a composer, these are not merely philosophical or metaphysical musings. These questions are inextricably tied to the actual daily experience of composition. Every artist knows the terrifying and crippling power of The Blank Page. *How can I possibly bring something out of nothing?* And then, as every artist also knows, once you've made the monumental effort to produce that *something*, you inevitably ask yourself, *how do I know whether or not it's good?* This is a very real, and often very bitter, struggle for me, and I know it is for others as well. For myself, I've discovered that the way forward is actually encapsulated in some way in the very first words of Genesis, quoted in the epigraph above. The first task is just to put something—*anything*—on the page, so that it's not blank anymore. *And God said, Let there be light.* Then, whatever I've put there, whether it's my own idea or someone else's, I accept it as it is and work with it—I don't change it or criticize it, at least not at first, but, rather, I allow it to suggest its own emergent forms and patterns. *And God saw the light, that it was good: and God divided the light from the darkness.* After discovering and rejoicing in the unique qualities of whatever I have to work with, I then gently start organizing it into clearer and clearer shapes and more and more meaningful forms. *And God called the light Day, and the darkness he called Night.* And finally, I have to decide to stop and move on to the next thing. *And the evening and morning were the first day.*

So perhaps this is the message of *Vespers*, this setting of the ancient evening office that begins each new day: from the descent into darkness comes a mysterious and gladsome light. Over the past two years of global pandemic—and the past two months of unfolding horror in Ukraine—with all the unresolvable complexities and knotty irregular rhythms that go along with such upheaval, I continue to hope that something new and bright and *good* may yet emerge from the darkness. I offer my piece, therefore, as a symbol of that hope, and as a token of encouragement for all those who strive towards the light.

Benedict Sheehan
April 2022

This note may be reproduced as required for programme notes.

Vespers was recorded in July 2021 at St. Stephen's Pro-Cathedral, Wilkes-Barre, Pennsylvania, by the Saint Tikhon Choir, under the direction of the composer. The recording is available from Cappella Records (CR423). The work as a whole is dedicated to Archimandrite Sergius, Abbot of St. Tikhon's Monastery.

Duration: *c*.60 minutes

Texts and Composer's Notes

Text translations by Donald Sheehan (1940–2010) used by permission of Wipf and Stock Publishers, www.wipfandstock.com. Texts from 'Hieratikon: Office Book for Priest and Deacon', Hierodeacon Herman and Vitaly Permiakov: editors, South Canaan, Penn. © St. Tikhon's Monastery Press, 2014.

1. The Opening Psalm

Psalm 103 LXX (104), translated by Donald Sheehan.

The first psalm of vespers, recounting the creation of the world and glorifying God for his mighty works. Based on a bold and lively irregular-meter chant from the ancient Valaam Monastery founded in the 14th century on the shores of Lake Ladoga. My choral setting of the entire 35-line psalm—the first of its kind in the Orthodox tradition—uses material from the original chant melody throughout, but with extensive composed additions and modifications.

Bless the Lord, O my soul.
Blessed art thou, O Lord.
O Lord my God, how magnificently dost thou exist, clothed in thanksgiving and majesty,
arrayed in light as with a garment, stretching out the heavens like a curtain.
He covers his high halls with the waters, appointing the clouds for his staircase, ascending on the wings of the wind,
Making his angels his spirits, his ministers a flame of fire.
He established earth on her sure foundations, she shall never give way unto ages of ages.
Blessed art thou, O Lord.
The deep like a garment is his clothing, the waters shall stand upon the mountains.
At thy rebuke they shall flee, at the crash of thy thunder, they shall tremble with fear.
The mountains rise up, the valleys sink down to the place thou hast founded for them.
Wondrous are thy works, O Lord.
Thou didst set a boundary never to be passed, the waters shall never again cover the earth.
Sending the springs into the valleys, he shall make the waters flow between the mountains.
He shall give water to every beast, the wild asses shall quench their thirst.
The birds of heaven shall dwell by them, from amidst the rocks they shall sing forth.
He waters the mountains from his upper chambers. The earth shall be satisfied with the fruit of thy works.
Growing the grass for the cattle, raising green plants to serve man, he brings forth bread from the earth
And wine to gladden man's heart, oil to make bright his face and bread to strengthen his heart.
The trees of the plain shall be fed, the cedars of Lebanon which thou didst plant.
In them shall the sparrows make nests, the heron's home greatest among them.
On the high hills are the deer, the cliffs are a refuge for the hyrax.[1]
He made the moon to mark seasons, the sun knows the time to set.
Thou makest darkness and it is night when all the forest beasts will prowl,
The young lions roaring for their prey, seeking their food from God.
When the sun rises, they will gather and lie down in their dens.
Man shall go out to his work and shall labor until the evening.
O Lord, how manifold are thy works, in wisdom hast thou made them all.
The earth is filled with thy creations,
As is this great and spacious sea that teems with countless things, living things both small and great.

There the ships ply their way, there is that Leviathan[2] that thou madest to play there.

All of them look to thee alone to give them food in due season.

When thou givest they shall gather in, when thou openest thy hands everything shall be filled with goodness.

But when thou turnest thy face away they shall be deeply troubled, when thou takest their breath away they shall die back again to dust.

Thou shalt send forth thy Spirit and they shall be created, thou shalt renew the face of the earth.

May the Lord's glory endure forever; the Lord shall be glad in his works.

He gazes on the earth and it trembles, he touches the mountains and they smoke.

I will sing to the Lord all my life, I will sing psalms to my God for as long as I have being.

May my thoughts be pleasing to him, and I shall be glad in the Lord.

May the sinners vanish from the earth, may the wicked wholly cease to be.

Bless the Lord, O my soul.

Glory to thee, O Lord, who hast made them all.

Glory to the Father and to the Son and to the Holy Spirit. Both now and ever and unto ages of ages. Amen.

Alleluia, alleluia, alleluia, glory to thee, O God. (*Thrice*)

[1]*hyrax* = small, herbivorous mammal; [2]*Leviathan* = a sea creature of enormous size, such as a whale

2. Great Litany

Texts from the Hieratikon (Office Book for Priest and Deacon), ed. by B. Sheehan.

Beginning with the words 'in peace let us pray to the Lord,' the responsorial *Great Litany* begins all of the major sung services in Orthodox worship. Here I take the unprecedented step of precisely notating the complex speech rhythms typical of Eastern Orthodox clerical chanting. A gentle and subdued setting with simple choral refrains, the *Great Litany* should allow the listener to meditate and enter a space of inner peace and calm.

Deacon: In peace let us pray to the Lord.

Singers: Lord, have mercy. (*After each petition*)

For the peace from above and for the salvation of our souls, let us pray to the Lord.

For the peace of the whole world, for the welfare of the holy churches of God, and for the union of all, let us pray to the Lord.

For this holy house and for those who enter it with faith, reverence, and the fear of God, let us pray to the Lord.

For the honorable priesthood, the diaconate in Christ, and for all the clergy and the people, let us pray to the Lord.

For this country, for all civil authorities, and for those who serve, let us pray to the Lord.

For this city, for every city and countryside, and for the faithful dwelling in them, let us pray to the Lord.

For seasonable weather, for abundance of the fruits of the earth, and for peaceful times, let us pray to the Lord.

For travelers by land, by sea, and by air; for the sick and the suffering; for captives and their salvation, let us pray to the Lord.

That we may be delivered from all affliction, wrath, danger, and necessity, let us pray to the Lord.

Help us, save us, have mercy on us, and keep us, O God, by thy grace.

Commemorating our most holy, most pure, most blessed and glorious Lady Theotokos and Ever-Virgin Mary with all the saints, (Most Holy Theotokos, save us)

Let us commend ourselves and each other, and all our life unto Christ our God.
Singers: To thee, O Lord.
Priest: For unto thee are due all glory, honor, and worship, to the Father and to the Son and to the Holy Spirit, now and ever and unto ages of ages.
Singers: Amen.

3. Blessed is the man

Selected verses from Psalms 1, 2, and 3, translated by Donald Sheehan.
Based on an obscure but majestic medieval Dormition Cathedral chant, my setting is inspired by the harmonic language of 17th-century *znamenny* polyphony, a fascinating body of harmonized chants that predates the wholesale adoption of European-style part writing in Russia.

Trio: Blessed is the man who walks not in the counsel of the ungodly.
Singers: Alleluia. (*After each petition*)
For the Lord knows the way of the righteous, and the way of the ungodly shall perish.
Serve the Lord with fear and rejoice in him with trembling.
Blessed are all they that put their trust in him.
Arise, O Lord, save me, O my God.
Salvation is from the Lord and thy blessing is upon thy people.
Glory to the Father and to the Son and to the Holy Spirit.
Now and ever and unto ages of ages. Amen.
Alleluia, alleluia, alleluia, glory to thee, O God. (*Thrice*)

4. Small Litany

Essentially an abbreviated reprise of the *Great Litany*, the *Small Litany* allows the listener once again to pause and meditate before diving into the more intense movements that follow.

Deacon: Again and again in peace, let us pray to the Lord.
Singers: Lord, have mercy. (*After each petition*)
Help us, save us, have mercy on us, and keep us, O God, by thy grace.
Commemorating our most holy, most pure, most blessed and glorious Lady Theotokos and Ever-Virgin Mary with all the saints, (Most Holy Theotokos, save us)
Let us commend ourselves and each other, and all our life unto Christ our God.
Singers: To thee, O Lord.
Priest: For unto thee are due all glory, honor, and worship, to the Father and to the Son and to the Holy Spirit, now and ever and unto ages of ages.
Singers: Amen.

5. The Lamp-lighting Psalms

Psalms 140 and 141 LXX (141 and 142), translated by Donald Sheehan.
The *Lamp-lighting Psalms* are the psalms of evening worship, going back even to ancient Temple worship in Jerusalem. They still form the centerpiece of the Orthodox evening office today, though they are typically only read aloud by a reader and are often significantly abbreviated. My setting, inspired by motifs from Byzantine chant, First Mode, uses an ancient responsorial form for psalm-singing with a gently repeated

choral refrain of 'Hear me, O Lord'. As far as I know, it is the first-ever through-composed setting of the *Lamp-lighting Psalms* in the Orthodox musical tradition.

Psalm 140: A psalm of David
Soloist: O Lord, I called upon thee, hear me.
Chorus: Hear me, O Lord. (*After each verse*)
O Lord, I called upon thee, hear me, receive the voice of my prayer when I call upon thee.
Let my prayer arise in thy sight as incense, let the lifting up of my hands be an evening sacrifice.
Set a guard, O Lord, over my mouth, a strong door about my lips.
Incline not my heart to evil words that ease the way for evil men to work their wicked deeds; let me not join their inner circles.
The righteous man shall chastise me with sweet mercy, and correct me, but the sweet oil of sinners shall never touch my head, for my prayer shall continually be against their delights.
Their judges were smashed on the rock, although they had heard my words, heard how sweet they were.
Their bones were all scattered in Hades, like an earth-clod broken on the earth.
For my eyes, O Lord, Lord, look to thee, in thee have I hoped, let not my soul slip away.
Preserve me from the snares they have set out for me, from the stumbling block set out for me by the workers of wickedness.
Let the wicked fall into their own nets, all of them together, while I alone pass through.

Psalm 141: Instruction by David, when he was in the cave, praying
With my voice I cried out to the Lord, with my voice I prayed to the Lord.
Before him I shall pour out my prayer, in his presence declare my afflictions.
When my spirit fainted within me, then thou knewest my paths, for on the way I was going they had hidden a snare for me.
I looked on the right, and I saw that no one had recognized me,
that all flight had failed me, that no one saw deeply my soul.
I cried out to thee, O Lord, saying: Thou art my hope, my share in the land of the living.
Attend unto my prayer for I am brought very low, free me from my tormentors for they are stronger than I.
Soloist: Bring my soul out of prison, O Lord,
Chorus: that I may sing praise to thy name.

6. Stikhira of the Resurrection

Text from the Octoechos (Book of Eight Tones), attributed to St John of Damascus (c.675–749), and Anatolius of Constantinople (5th cent.), translated by Anon., with interpolated verses from Psalm 129 (130), translated by Donald Sheehan.

The *Stikhira of the Resurrection* are hymns from Saturday evening vespers, First Mode, celebrating the Resurrection of Christ, woven into the concluding verses of the *Lamp-lighting Psalms*. My musical setting is inspired by motifs from Byzantine chant, motifs that evolve gradually from unison melodies over a pedal tone—a texture typical of Byzantine music—into a triumphant multi-part choral texture in the movement's final sections. To my knowledge, it is the first through-composed choral setting of these hymns in English.

First Stikhiron: Accept our evening prayers, O holy Lord. Grant us remission of sins, for thou alone hast revealed the Resurrection to the world.
Verse: The righteous shall patiently wait until thou shalt deal richly with me.
Second Stikhiron: Encircle Zion and surround her, O people. Give glory in her to the One who rose from

the dead. For he is our God, who has delivered us from our transgressions.

Verse: From out of the depths, O Lord, I have cried out to thee, O Lord, hear my voice.

Third Stikhiron: Come, O people, let us hymn and fall down before Christ, glorifying his resurrection from the dead. For he is our God, who has delivered the world from the enemy's deceit.

Verse: Let thine ears be attentive to the voice of my supplications.

Fourth Stikhiron: Be glad, O heavens! Sound trumpets, O foundations of the earth! Sing in gladness, O mountains! Behold, Emmanuel has nailed our sins to the Cross; granting life, he has slain death. He has resurrected Adam as the Lover of man.

Verse: If thou, Lord, shouldst mark iniquities, O Lord, who could stand? For with thee is forgiveness.

Fifth Stikhiron: Let us praise him who was willingly crucified in the flesh for our sake. He suffered and was buried, but rose again from the dead. By orthodoxy confirm thy Church, O Christ. Grant peace for our life as the gracious Lover of man.

Verse: For thy name's sake, O Lord, I have patiently waited for thee, my soul went on patiently waiting for thy word, my soul has hoped in the Lord.

Sixth Stikhiron: We stand unworthily before thy life-bearing tomb, O Christ God, offering glory to thine unspeakable compassion. Thou hast accepted the Cross and death, O Sinless One, to grant the world resurrection as the Lover of man.

Verse: From the morning watch until night, let Israel hope in the Lord.

Seventh Stikhiron: Let us praise the Word, coeternal with the Father. He ineffably came forth from the virginal womb. He freely accepted the Cross and death for our sake. He was raised in glory. Glory to thee, O lifegiving Lord, the Savior of our souls.

Verse: Glory to the Father and to the Son and to the Holy Spirit. Now and ever and unto ages of ages. Amen.

Dogmatikon: Let us praise the Virgin Mary, the gate of heaven, the glory of the world, the song of angels, the beauty of the faithful. She was born of man, yet gave birth to God. She was revealed as heaven, as the temple of the Godhead. She destroyed the wall of enmity. She commenced the peace, she opened the kingdom. Since she is our foundation of faith, our defender is the Lord whom she bore: Courage, courage, O people of God, for Christ will destroy our enemies, since he is all powerful.

7. O gladsome Light

Text from the Horologion (Book of the Hours), translated by Anon.

O gladsome Light (Φῶς Ἱλαρόν, Lumen Hilare) is one of the oldest Christian hymns, dating from the late 3rd century or perhaps even earlier. My setting is based on Byzantine chant, Mode 1 Plagal (Mode 5). The chant is sung here by a soprano soloist, perhaps giving the sense that the Virgin Mary—herself the subject of the hymn immediately preceding this movement—is now singing to Christ. This is the central movement of *Vespers*, both structurally and dramatically.

O gladsome Light of the holy glory of the immortal Father, heavenly, holy, blessed, O Jesus Christ: now that we have come to the setting of the sun, and behold the light of evening, we praise God: Father, Son, and Holy Spirit. For meet it is at all times to worship thee with voices of praise, O Son of God and Giver of life; therefore all the world doth glorify thee.

8. The Lord is King

Psalm 92 LXX (93), translated by Donald Sheehan.

A *prokimenon*, an antiphonal psalm meant to introduce a scripture reading, this exuberant setting is inspired by the Baroque-style melodies of the Kyiv Caves Monastery, thus turning a normally simple bit of responsory into a mini-concerto for alto and chorus.

Soloist: The evening prokimenon in the Sixth Tone: The Lord is King, he is robed in majesty.
Chorus: The Lord is King, he is robed in majesty.
Soloist: The Lord is robed in strength and has girded himself, for he has established our lands so that they shall never be shaken.
From of old is thy throne prepared, from all eternity thou art.
The rivers, O Lord, have lifted up, the rivers have uplifted their voices, the rivers shall raise their strong floods with the voices of many waves.
Wondrous is the surging of the sea, wondrous is the Lord on high.
Thy testimonies were steadfastly made, holiness befits thy house, O Lord, unto length of days.

9. Evening Prayer

Text from the Horologion (Book of the Hours), translated by Anon.
A gentle and subdued setting of the vespers prayer 'Vouchsafe, O Lord'. This movement works particularly well as a stand-alone anthem.

Vouchsafe, O Lord, to keep us this evening without sin. Blessed art thou, O Lord, God of our fathers, and praised and glorified is thy Name forever. Amen.
Let thy mercy, O Lord, be upon us, as we have set our hope on thee.
Blessed art thou, O Lord, teach me thy statutes.
Blessed art thou, O Master, make me to understand thy commandments.
Blessed art thou, O Holy One, enlighten me with thy precepts.
Thy mercy, O Lord, endureth forever: despise not the works of thy hands.
To thee is due praise, to thee is due song, to thee is due glory: to the Father and to the Son and to the Holy Spirit, now and ever and unto ages of ages. Amen.

10. The Song of Simeon

Luke 2: 29–32 (King James Version).
The Nunc Dimittis. A solemn song of departure at the end of vespers, the *Song of Simeon* combines a well-known chant melody (Tone 8, 'Behold, the Bridegroom'), used by both Gretchaninoff and Rimsky-Korsakov in their settings of Passion Week, with a freely composed part for basso profundo. My setting is, I believe, the only work for basso profundo solo in Orthodox literature in English. It is dedicated to the great American profundo Glenn Miller.

Lord, now lettest thou thy servant depart in peace according to thy word. For mine eyes have seen thy salvation, which thou hast prepared before the face of all people: a light to enlighten the Gentiles, and the glory of thy people Israel.

Interlude: The Trisagion Prayers

Text from the Horologion (Book of the Hours), translated by Anon.
A set of frequently recited prayers, appointed for nearly every Orthodox service and personal prayer rule. This section may be omitted during concert performance, if desired, but it provides a welcome moment of reflection and repose before the intensity of the final two movements.

Reader: Holy God, Holy Mighty, Holy Immortal, have mercy on us. (*Thrice*)

Glory to the Father and to the Son and to the Holy Spirit, now and ever and unto ages of ages. Amen.

All-holy Trinity, have mercy on us: Lord, cleanse us from our sins; Master, pardon our transgressions; Holy One, visit and heal our infirmities for thy name's sake.

Lord, have mercy. (*Thrice*)

Glory to the Father and to the Son and to the Holy Spirit, now and ever and unto ages of ages. Amen.

Our Father, who art in heaven, hallowed be thy name. Thy kingdom come. Thy will be done on earth as it is in heaven. Give us this day our daily bread, and forgive us our trespasses as we forgive those who trespass against us. And lead us not into temptation, but deliver us from the evil one.

Priest: For thine is the kingdom, and the power, and the glory, of the Father and of the Son and of the Holy Spirit, now and ever and unto ages of ages.

Reader: Amen.

11. Rejoice, O Virgin

Text from the Horologion (Book of the Hours), translated by Anon.

The *Ave Maria*. A hymn to the Virgin Mary sung at the conclusion of vespers, my setting is based on a little-known chant of the Monastery of St Cyril on the White Lake (*Kirillo-Belozersky*). The plaintive, wandering, melismatic chant is arranged in a dense and shimmering choral texture and conjures up a feeling of mystery and awe at the Incarnation of Christ. My setting is, as far as I know, the only choral arrangement of this particular chant.

Rejoice, O Virgin Theotokos, Mary full of grace, the Lord is with thee. Blessed art thou among women, and blessed is the fruit of thy womb, for thou hast borne the Savior of our souls.

12. The Closing Psalm

Psalm 33 LXX (34), translated by Donald Sheehan.

Using the same Valaam chant melody from the first movement, I bookend my *Vespers* with a complex multi-section setting of the final psalm of vespers. As the piece develops, the motifs of Valaam Chant subtly evolve into melodies reminiscent of American folk music, thereby drawing a connection between the past, present, and future of Orthodox liturgical music in America. The movement's ecstatic final section in 7/8 time completes an unanswered cadence from the first movement, thus giving the whole work a kind of internal unity.

I will bless the Lord at all times, his praise shall continually be in my mouth.

My soul shall be praised in the Lord, the meek shall hear of it and be glad.

O magnify the Lord with me, and let us exalt his name together.

I sought the Lord and he heard me, and delivered me from all my afflictions.

Come close to him and be illumined, and your countenance shall never be shamed.

This poor man cried out and the Lord heard him, and saved him out of all his troubles.

The angel of the Lord shall encamp around those who fear him, and deliver them.

O taste and see that the Lord is good; blessed is the man who puts his hope in him.

Fear the Lord, you his saints, there is no want to those who fear him.

Rich men have turned poor and starved, but those who seek the Lord shall not lack any good things.

Come, children, listen to me, I will teach you the fear of the Lord.

Who is the man who desires life, who loves to behold good days?

Keep your tongue from evil and your lips from speaking deceit.

Depart from evil and do good; seek peace and pursue it.

The eyes of the Lord are on the righteous, his ears are open to their supplications.

The Lord's countenance is upon evildoers, to uproot their remembrance from the earth.

The righteous cry out and the Lord hears and delivers them out of all their troubles.

The Lord is near those shattered in heart, the humbled in spirit he will save.

Many are the troubles of the righteous, but the Lord delivers them out of them all.

The Lord shall guard all their bones, not one of them shall be broken.

The death of sinners is evil, and those hating the righteous shall go wrong.

The Lord will redeem the souls of his servants, and none will go wrong who put their hope in him.

Glory to the Father and to the Son and to the Holy Spirit, both now and ever and unto ages of ages. Amen.

Alleluia, alleluia, alleluia, glory to thee, O God.

For Fr. Sergius
A Servant of Beauty
This work is further dedicated to all those who, in their art and in their lives,
respect the inherent freedom of every person and who cherish the beauty of every living thing.

VESPERS

BENEDICT SHEEHAN

1. The Opening Psalm

Psalm 103 (104),
trans. Donald Sheehan (1940–2010)

Based on Valaam chant

OXFORD UNIVERSITY PRESS, MUSIC DEPARTMENT, GREAT CLARENDON STREET, OXFORD OX2 6DP

ag - es of ag - es.

ag - es of ag - es. Bless - ed art thou, O Lord.

ag - es of ag - es. Bless - ed art thou, O Lord.

ag - es of ag - es. Bless - ed art thou, O Lord.

ag - es of ag - es. Bless - ed art thou, O Lord.

The deep like a gar - ment is his cloth - ing, the wa - ters shall stand up -

The deep like a gar - ment is his cloth - ing, the wa - ters shall stand up - on the

The deep like a gar - ment is his cloth - ing, the wa - ters shall stand up - on the

8

¹*hyrax* = small, herbivorous mammal

count-less things, liv-ing things both small and great.

There the ships

Who hast made them all,

made them all,

Who hast made them all,

made them all,

ply their way,___ there is that Le-vi-a-than[1] that thou mad-est to play there.___

glo-ry to thee, O Lord, who hast made them

glo -

glo -

[1] *Leviathan* = a sea creature of enormous size, such as a whale

* Do not sound the final consonants.

* Do not sound the final consonants.

2. *Great Litany*

Text from the Hieratikon (Office Book for Priest and Deacon)

Text from 'Hieratikon: Office Book for Priest and Deacon', Hierodeacon Herman and Vitaly Permiakov: editors. South Canaan, Penn. © St. Tikhon's Monastery Press, 2014

peace of the whole world, for the wel-fare of the ho-ly church-es of God, and for the u-nion of

all, let us pray to the Lord. For this ho-ly house and for

Lord, have mer-cy.

Lord, have mer-cy.

Lord, have mer-cy.

Lord, have mer-cy.

those who en-ter it with faith, re-v'rence, and the fear of God,___ let us pray to the Lord.___

___ For the ho-n'ra-ble priest-hood,___ the di-a-co-nate in Christ,___ and for

Lord, have mer - cy.

Lord, have mer - cy.

Lord, have mer - cy.

Lord, have mer - cy.

all the cler - gy and the peo - ple,___ let us pray to the Lord.___ For

Lord, have mer - cy.

Lord, have mer - cy.___

Lord, have mer - cy.___

Lord, have mer - cy.___

this coun - try,___ for all ci - vil au - tho - ri - ties,___ and for those who serve,___ let us pray to the Lord.

-bun - dance of the fruits of the earth,_____ and for peace - ful times,_____ let us pray to the Lord._____

_____ Lord, have mer - cy._____

Lord, have mer - cy._____

Lord, have mer - cy._____

Lord, have mer - cy._____

For tra - vel - ers by land, by sea, and by air;_____ for the sick and the suf - fer - ing;_____ for

thee are due all glo - ry, ho - nor, and wor - ship, __ to the Fa - ther and to the Son and to the Ho - ly

Spi - rit, now and ev - er and un - to ag - es of ag - es. __

A - men.
A - men.
A - men.
A - men.

3. Blessed is the man

Text from Psalms 1–3,
trans. Donald Sheehan (1940–2010)

Based on Dormition Cathedral chant

36

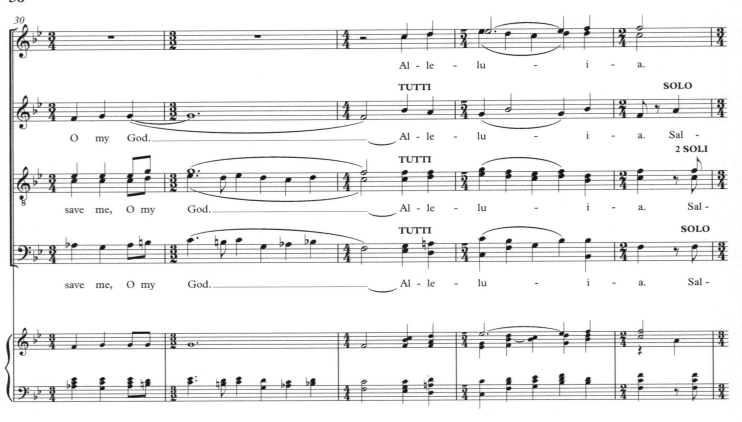

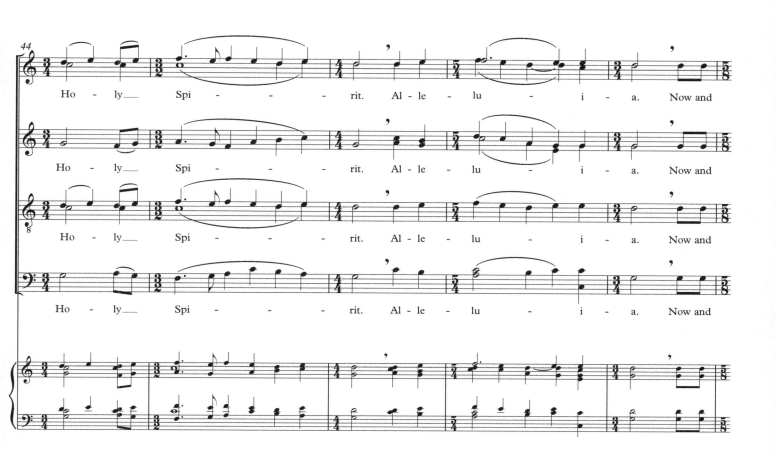

4. Small Litany

Text from the Hieratikon (Office Book for Priest and Deacon)

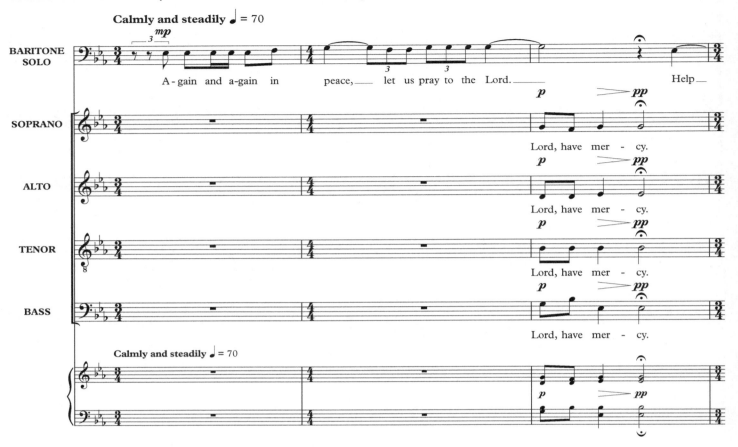

Text from 'Hieratikon: Office Book for Priest and Deacon', Hierodeacon Herman and Vitaly Permiakov: editors. South Canaan, Penn. © St. Tikhon's Monastery Press, 2014

-mend our-selves and each o-ther, and all our life_____ un-to Christ our God._____

To thee,_____ O

To thee,_____ O

To thee, O

To thee,_____ O

For un-to thee are due all glo-ry, ho-nor, and wor-ship, to the

Lord.

Lord.

Lord.

Lord.

Fa - ther and to the Son and to the Ho - ly Spi - rit, now and ev - er and un - to

poco rit.

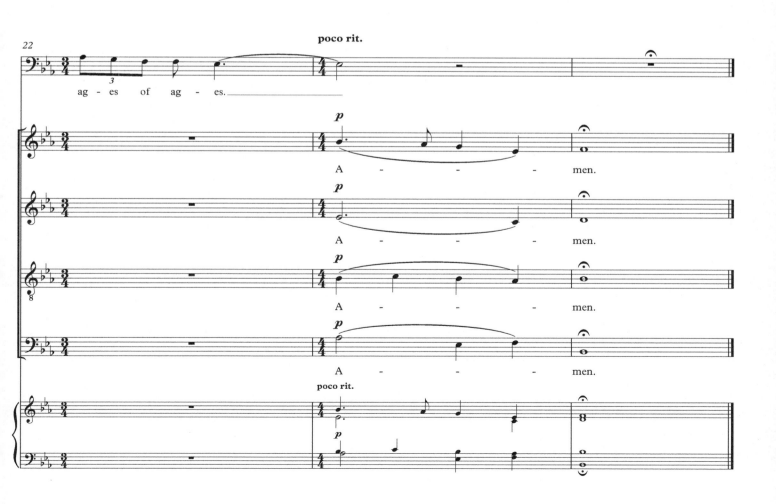

ag - es of ag - es.

A - - - men.

A - - - men.

A - - - men.

A - - - men.

5. The Lamp-lighting Psalms

Psalms 140 (141) and 141 (142),
trans. Donald Sheehan (1940–2010)

Based on motifs from Byzantine chant, First Mode

SEMI-CHORUS (1–3 singers per part)

In - cline not my heart to e - vil

SEMI-CHORUS (1–3 singers per part)

Set a guard, O Lord, o - ver my mouth, a strong door a - bout my lips.

Hear me, O Lord.

Hear me, O Lord.

Hear me, O Lord.

Hear me, O Lord.

words that ease the way for e - vil men to work their wic - ked deeds; let me not join their in - ner

attacca

6. Stikhira of the Resurrection

Text from the Octoechos (Book of Eight Tones),
attrib. St John of Damascus (c.675–749)
and Anatolius of Constantinople (5th cent.), trans. Anon.,
and Psalm 129 (130), trans. Donald Sheehan (1940–2010)

Based on motifs from Byzantine chant, First Mode,
combined with themes from Znamenny chant

3 BARITONE SOLI

-pas - sion. Thou hast ac - cept - ed the Cross and death, O Sin - less One, to grant the

oh

oh

SOPRANO SOLO

From the morn - ing watch __ un - til

world re - sur - rec - tion as the Lov - er __ of man.

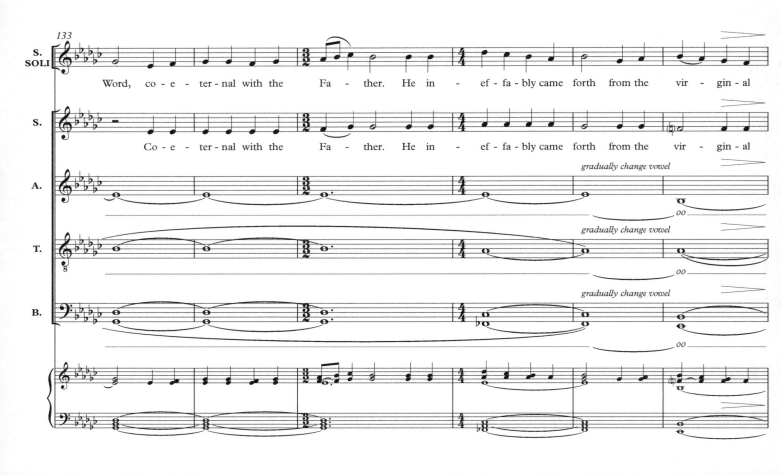

Let us praise_____ the Vir-gin___ Ma - ry, the gate of hea-ven, the glo-ry of__the world, the

song_____ of an - gels, the beau-ty of the faith-ful.   mm_____

She was born_____ of

She was born of

She was born of

7. O gladsome Light

Text from the Horologion (Book of the Hours)
trans. Anon.

Based on a Byzantine melody

8. The Lord is King

Psalm 92 (93),
trans. Donald Sheehan (1940–2010)

Based on a melody from the Kyiv Caves Monastery

9. Evening Prayer

Text from the Horologion (Book of the Hours),
trans. Anon.

Bless-ed art thou, O Ho-ly One, en - light-en me_____ with thy pre-cepts. Thy mer - cy, O Lord, en-dur-eth for-

Bless-ed art thou, O Ho-ly One, en - light - en me__ with thy pre-cepts. Thy mer - cy, O Lord, en-dur-eth for-

Bless-ed art thou, O Ho-ly One, en - light - en me__ with thy pre-cepts. Thy mer - cy, O Lord, en-dur-eth for-

Bless-ed art thou, O Ho-ly One, en - light - en me__ with thy pre-cepts. Thy mer - cy, O Lord, en-dur-eth for-

- ev - er: des - pise not the works of thy hands. To thee_____ is due praise, to thee_____ is due song, to

- ev - er: des - pise not the works of thy hands. To thee_____ is due praise, to thee_____ is due song, to

- ev - er: des - pise not the works of thy hands. To thee is due praise, to thee is due song, to

- ev - er: des - pise not the works of thy hands. To thee is due praise, to thee is due song, to

thee _____ is due glo-ry: to the Fa-ther ___ and to the Son ___ and to the Ho - ly

thee _____ is due glo-ry: to the Fa-ther ___ and to the Son ___ and to the Ho - ly

thee ___ is due glo - ry: to the Fa-ther ___ and to the Son ___ and to the Ho - ly

thee ___ is due glo - ry: to the Fa-ther ___ and to the Son ___ and to the Ho - ly

Spi-rit, ___ now and ev-er ___ and un-to ag-es of ag - es. A - - - men.

Spi-rit, ___ now and ev-er ___ and un-to ag-es of ag - es. A - - - men.

Spi-rit, ___ now and ev-er ___ and un-to ag-es of ag - es. A - - - men.

Spi-rit, ___ now and ev-er ___ and un-to ag-es of ag - es. A - - - men.

for Glenn Miller

10. The Song of Simeon

(original key)

Luke 2: 29–32 (King James Version)

Based on Tone 8 'Behold, the Bridegroom'

for Glenn Miller

10a. The Song of Simeon

(higher key)

Luke 2: 29–32 (King James Version)

Based on Tone 8 'Behold, the Bridegroom'

Interlude: The Trisagion Prayers

Text from the Horologion (Book of the Hours),
trans. Anon.

11. Rejoice, O Virgin

Text from the Horologion (Book of the Hours), trans. Anon.

Based on a chant of the Monastery of St Cyril on the White Lake

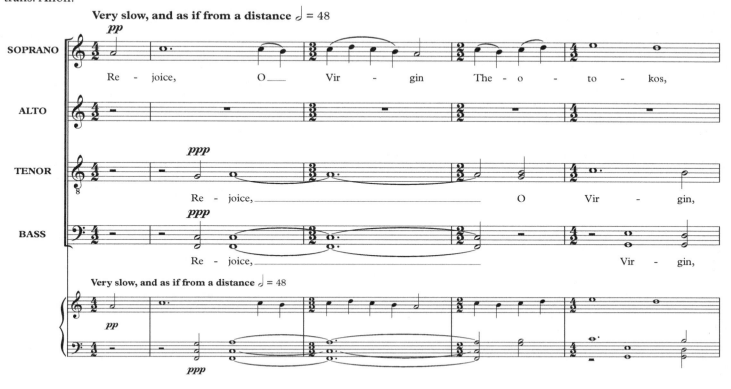

12. The Closing Psalm

Psalm 33 (34),
trans. Donald Sheehan (1940–2010)

Based on motifs from Valaam chant

© Oxford University Press 2022
Text translations by Donald Sheehan used by permission of Wipf and Stock Publishers, www.wipfandstock.com

JJ